So You're Gonna Be A DAD – Now What?

So You're Gonna Be A DAD
– Now What?

building hope & endurance
for the new father

Scott Patchin

Scott Patchin

credo
house publishers

Published in the United States by Credo House Publishers,
a division of Credo Communications, LLC, Grand Rapids, Michigan.
www.credohousepublishers.net

To respond to the message of this book, for more information about the author's
speaking schedule, and for details on how to order additional copies of
So You're Gonna Be A Dad—Now What? please contact the author at

Email: scott@momentsforfathers.com

World Wide Web: www.momentsforfathers.com

ISBN: 978-0-9787620-6-3

Editor: Mike Vander Klipp
Proofreader: Tim Hill
Cover design: Sherri Days
Interior design and composition: Sharon VanLoozenoord

Printed in the United States of America

10 9 8 7 6 5 4 3 2 1

First Edition

This book was made to be written in— and it starts here!

IF THIS IS A GIFT—For a son, son-in-law, husband, brother, or friend, use this space to share your perspectives on fatherhood—share a war story, or tell the recipient why you think he will be a great father.

IF YOU PURCHASED THIS BOOK FOR YOURSELF—Use this space to record three things that most excite you about being a father as well as your three greatest fears.

_____

_____

_____

_____

_____

_____

_____

_____

_____

_____

_____

_____

_____

_____

_____

_____

Contents

ON BEING A BETTER SPOUSE

ON BEING A BETTER SON OR SON-IN-LAW

ON SURVIVING

For Jenny
my love, my wife, my friend

For Ben, Ana, Mia, and Aubrey
my teachers

Introduction

So you're going to be a dad. Or perhaps you just became one. I've been where you are a few times—four to be exact. I've been the panicked husband headed to the hospital trying to act in control, with the needle on the speedometer and my tight grip on the steering wheel telling a different story. I've practically worn out my snooze alarm in my attempts to make up for a sleepless night and postpone work for a few extra minutes. I've faced the mustard-colored masses on the south side of the diaper. I have collapsed, more than once, filled with wonder at how a tiny little ten-pound human being could whip a full-grown man into submission.

One day in June 1995 I woke up and I was a dad. Each day since that moment I have learned something new about dadhood . . . sometimes the hard way, sometimes the easy way. When I look back at all of my experiences during the first two years as a father, one thing I wish I had was someone to provide a few bits of wisdom for me along the way. You know, someone to reinforce my frustrations, to sympathize with my sacrifices, and to tell me I wasn't the only one who thought I was going crazy. That's what this book is designed to be—an offering of some of those bits of wisdom around some of the fatherhood "moments" that I have experienced.

Imagine that you're lifting a heavy rock or moving some broken concrete to another area of your yard. What would it feel like after the first step? The second step? Would you have to put it down? If your mom wasn't around with a bar of soap to wash out your mouth, what words would you use to describe the experience? Being a dad is a little bit like heavy lifting, sometimes we need help. After we've moved a few chunks of concrete and hefted some boulders, we learn how it can be done faster and with less effort. This book is some of my learning, but it will become your book when the empty spaces I have provided start filling up. More to follow on making this book your own.

How to Use This Book

My father once told me not to dog-ear the pages of a book because it damages the book. That's good advice when you have to face a stern librarian, but it's exactly the wrong advice for this book! This book is designed to stay with you, the owner, for a long time. Use it to capture those moments of fatherhood where you learn something you want to remember—even some that you might want to forget, but the smell is etched into your brain. There are places to jot notes at the end of each chapter, and at the end of the book there are blank pages for you to add your own stories.

ON BEING
A BETTER DAD

Sometimes You Just Have to Laugh

ONE DAY, WHEN MY oldest son was eighteen months old, I noticed a familiar redness coming into his cheeks and saw his clenched jaw—you'll soon peg this as an indicator of a soon-to-be soiled diaper. Jenny and I were in the middle of an actual adult conversation with my parents, so I excused myself and decided to try a quick change using the old "standup" diaper-changing method. Note that this method is almost never used by moms, but it is regularly employed by dads who think they can accomplish the impossible. For the rookie father, this is an advanced move that allows parents to change the diaper without laying the child down. I urge you not to try this until your child:

    a) can stand (sorry for stating the obvious, but I have visions of your trying this with a newborn and my getting a nasty email from your wife).

    b) understands and can execute the command to "stay standing and don't move!"

Back to the story. My son and I quickly ran to the bathroom and my vision of a sub-sixty-second procedure started out as a promising proposition. My son was cooperating, and all the materials (wipes, diapers) were in their normal places.

In a flash, the plan quickly went down the tubes . . . the first diaper was already off, the clean diaper was not yet ready, and my boy still wasn't done. Grimacing with effort, I saw that he was working up another surprise for Daddy. The next few seconds were a blur, but as I assessed the situation I quickly identified the single biggest threat to my quick-change plan—the white shag rug he was standing on. The simple equation here was:

poop + carpet = cleanup
cleanup = delay (angry me) + stain (annoyed wife)

I was going beyond the standard male measure of "the dirt you can't see can't hurt you, as long as it doesn't stink." With the deftness of a goalie trying to preserve a Stanley Cup victory by stopping a sizzling slapshot, I stuck out my hand, turned my head, and made the save. When it was over, I looked at him, he looked at me, and we both started laughing.

Becoming a parent doesn't tie you into any protected union, and there's no contract to sign when the baby comes home. If there were, I'm sure the scene I just described would be abolished by some sort of non-gross-out clause. Every now and then you encounter those unique moments in parenting when you just have to laugh. I'm not sure if it's because laughter is often great therapy (and free!) or because there's just no place else to go. In this scenario I could have been mad, frustrated, disgusted, _____ (you fill in the blank). But as a parent there are those situations that you find yourself in when you realize that you are the only person who is going to be able to fix it. When you get in one of those situations . . .

Remember, Dad, sometimes you just have to laugh.

Some questions to think about:

- ◆ *What kinds of things just completely turn your stomach?*

- ◆ *When is the last time you have had to "laugh off" a tough situation?*

your space   *notes . . . thoughts . . . musings . . .*

_____

_____

_____

_____

_____

_____

_____

_____

_____

_____

_____

_____

_____

_____

_____

_____

_____

_____

_____

_____

_____

_____

_____

_____

_____

_____

So, Are You Going to Sing?

I HAVE THIS RECURRING dream. Actually, it's more like a nightmare. My daughter asks me to sing a song at her wedding, and out of obligation I say yes. She picks a song that I used to do as a lullaby for all the kids, "Too-Ra-Loo-Ra-Loo-Ra" by Bing Crosby. As I stand up to sing, accompanied by music and with five hundred people watching me, I forget most of the words and the ones that do come out are off key. In my dream I'm genuinely confused, because it always sounded better in the rocking chair. What's more, it usually worked—the kids generally settled down with Dad's crooning. But I wake up remembering that I'm not a very good singer.

So, are you going to sing? Would you sing only if the house was empty? Would you sing if your friends were downstairs and within earshot? Would you sing if your wife could hear? All these questions to think about! But Dad, it's not about what you sing or how well you sing; it's about having the guts to forget who else is listening, and realizing that this is a concert for one little person who's not a very picky critic! Babies just love to hear the sound of your voice.

Being a father is sometimes just about participation—as you will learn later when you're asked to coach a sport you know nothing about! But for now, you're just being asked to create a noise that, when repeated nightly, will signal bedtime to this tiny person. It also communicates that dad is there, and he's not afraid to show his love through singing.

Call me partial, but I recommend "Too-Ra-Loo-Ra-Loo-Ra," downloadable from several sites on the Internet. If you are really hurting for material, try a classic like "Rock a Bye Baby" or "Take Me Out to the Ballgame" or "Mary Had a Little Lamb."

**Remember, Dad, the audience is one,
and the love is in the song, not the notes!**

Some questions to think about:

- ◆ *What song do you remember being sung to you as a child?*

- ◆ *Ask five dads what their favorite lullaby is and how often they sing it to their child?*

your space   *notes . . . thoughts . . . musings . . .*

You're Big, They're Little—
So Get Little

MY SON STARTED CRAWLING at about seven months old, about the same time most children do. One day I was standing there watching him crawl and he crawled up to my foot, used my leg to pull himself up to his knees and tilted his neck so he could look up at me. He gave me a big toothless, drooly smile, but just as soon as his head tilted back the weight of it threw off his balance. He toppled backwards, and his head hit the wood floor with a resounding "thump"! His broad smile quickly dissolved into tears, and the moment was over. As so often happens in parenting, I went from congratulating him to consoling him in an instant.

I am 6'3" tall and my top parenting weight was around 225 pounds, so unless I am at an NFL training camp, I'm considered to be relatively big. I can only imagine what I must look like from an ankle view. After seeing how happy my son was to climb up my leg for that brief moment, I decided to make it easier for him; I laid down on the floor. From that moment on I became a playground toy—a human jungle gym—to all of our children. When I was on the floor, they could climb onto my chest, over my legs, or onto my head. It was even funny how they would see me lie down and come scooting over because I was getting down to their level and becoming little, like them. While they couldn't rise to my level, I could certainly shrink to theirs!

We have to learn how to meet our kids where they are and engage them at their level. An index finger can become a wrestling mate for a three month old; repeatedly knocking down block towers can be a Godzilla movie to a nine month old; and a father lying on the floor can be a trip up Mount Everest to a twelve month old. We can look forward to the day when they can play in our world, but in the meantime, we can take time today to enter into theirs.

Remember, Dad, you're big, they're little—so get little.

Some questions to think about:

- *What person in your life did the best job of "entering your world" and not requiring you to come into theirs?*

- *What game do you look forward to playing with your child?*

11

your space   *notes . . . thoughts . . . musings . . .*

Life's Three Greatest Smells: Steak on the Grill, Mom's Apple Pie, and a Baby after a Bath

THERE ARE A FEW smells that I miss. My parents had lilac bushes in our back yard as I was growing up, and every spring they would bloom into incredible flower blossoms. I remember how I could smell those fragrant blooms from inside the house. I miss that smell. In college, when I wanted to unwind, I would head toward the waters of Lake Superior and spend some time facing the cool fresh breezes coming off the water. I miss that smell. When I lived in Chicago there was a late night burrito place called Taco Burrito Palace. About six hours after a big burrito, the effects of the meal started and my wife would yell at me. Okay, so maybe I don't miss that smell, and Jenny *really* doesn't miss it, but you get the idea.

When each of my children were babies, I looked forward to bathing them in their little mini tubs, wrapping them in towels, then picking up those squirmy infants and placing their fresh-washed heads onto my shoulder. Then I would put my nose right into their necks and take a deep breath—it was 100% baby and 100% perfect. I'm not sure if it was the soft skin, or the soap, or the fact that this was the only time during the day that they were clean. But man, what a great memory.

A parent bathing a child is a ritual—and since mine have grown, I haven't again had a chance to hold a baby after a bath. I can drive to a lake, find a lilac bush, or even make my own burrito—but that sweet smell after a bath will probably have to wait until I have grandchildren.

Remember, Dad, enjoy the smell while you can, because it will not last forever!

Some questions to think about:

♦ *Thinking back over your life, what are the greatest smells you can remember?*

♦ *Are there any that bring back memories when you encounter them today?*

your space   *notes . . . thoughts . . . musings . . .*

"Dad" Means Parent, Not Babysitter

OUR FIRST CHILD WAS three months old, and we were finally at the point where we dared to take him out in public. We had moved into a new house, were getting used to new neighbors, and we were dying for some interaction with trusted friends. Plus we had the need to prove to ourselves that our lives hadn't completely changed, that we could still pull off one of those pre-baby "road trips." So we made preparations to drive to our friend's house, have dinner, and even stay overnight.

While my friend and I enjoyed dinner and my son snoozed in his car seat, I heard our wives talking about how great it would be to get away for a few hours to catch a movie and do a little shopping—just so they could feel like normal people again. It was then that I hatched a plan designed to win me a few points and allow my friend and I a chance to watch the football game that was on that night! Feeling magnanimous, I said, "Hey, why don't the dads stay here and babysit these little bundles of joy while you two take a trip to the mall."

I expected to be praised as a hero, with my wife declaring to the world what a thoughtful and compassionate husband I was to volunteer my valuable time to care for our child while she got away from it all. But what I got was quite the opposite—something along the lines of a cold, hard stare from my wife, followed by this piercing comment from my friend's wife: "Babysit?" she said. "Aren't you the parent?" It was a lesson I would never forget—probably the single best "correction" I have ever received.

Just think of those two titles: Parent and Babysitter.

A Babysitter is one who completes a task and gets paid for it. At the end of the evening, when the job is done, the babysitter gets to put on her coat and go home. Success is measured only by whether the kids are in bed, how intact the house is at the end of the night, and how positive the stories are from the kids the next morning. The title of Parent, however, doesn't include a finish line. The rewards of being a parent aren't always immediately evident, and even though you might take a break here and there, you never really escape the responsibility that goes with it. But it's a title that you'll wear proudly, and wear for life.

I have a good friend who was dealing with a screaming ten week old. Both he and his wife were pretty frazzled. So I decided to take him to a movie to get his mind off it. On the way, as he was telling me about their struggles as new parents, I commented that I was surprised that he didn't search the Web (one of his favorite pastimes) to see if there was any free advice out there. His comment to me was,

"You don't understand. I do things in our house like the maintenance and finances. She's in charge of all the parenting things." It was a good time for me to pose the question, "Are you the babysitter or the parent?"

Remember, Dad, you're the parent, not the babysitter.

Some questions to think about:

- *What's your maximum time limit for fully focused parenting without a break?*

- *What distractions are so strong for you that when they're present you take your eye off the ball and switch into "babysitting" mode?*

your space *notes . . . thoughts . . . musings . . .*

_____

_____

_____

_____

_____

_____

_____

_____

_____

_____

_____

_____

_____

_____

_____

_____

_____

_____

_____

_____

_____

_____

_____

_____

Don't Hate the SuperDad

I LIVE NEAR A SuperDad. Now, he doesn't wear a shirt with a big S on the front, or shower me with advice when we talk, or display his "Father of the Year" awards on his mantle— but he is SuperDad.

How do I define a SuperDad? It's someone who puts a tremendous amount of energy into parenting, who always seems to be having "fun" with his kids, who never publicly loses his cool, and who your kids seem to want to play with more than you. That's SuperDad. Do you hate that guy or love that guy?

When the kids are under two, the SuperDad keeps his cool under intense pressure (hot days, diaper shortages, trapped in a crowd with a crying child) and he never seems to sweat. But I've been able to look behind the cape, and let me tell you a couple of secrets. First of all, they all sweat and get angry sometimes. Second, they are not trying to be SuperDad, they are just trying to be Dad. So, do you hate that guy or love that guy?

Love him or hate him, make sure you watch him. As dads, we can all learn from guys who seem to have worked out the secrets of patient and kind parenting. What drives him to do what he is doing? How does he see his role as a father and who does he look up to when he thinks of a great dad?

The SuperDad in my circle of friends has taught me a lot and I depend on him. First, he taught me that he's not perfect. He has bad days just like the rest of us, and there are certain situations that drive him crazy and cause him to lose his cool. The big thing he's taught me is to make play with my children a priority, to do things that include them, and to genuinely enjoy parenting. This means you smile, you laugh, and you bring energy to being a dad.

> **Remember, Dad, the big thing**
> **that SuperDad does well is openly show**
> **love and joy to his kids.**
> **You can be SuperDad, too!**

Some questions to think about:

- *What fathers do you admire because of how they are with their kids?*

- *What do you admire about what they do with their children?*

- *How would you want someone to answer the previous question if they were talking about you?*

your space   *notes . . . thoughts . . . musings . . .*

Where's the Job Description?

AFTER I ALREADY HAD three children, I was spending a weekend with a close friend and his family. I was changing the diaper of our youngest daughter, and as we talked about the kids he shared with me that he had changed very few diapers. Confused, I asked him what "very few" meant. He just kind of threw out his answer: "Oh, about once a month, and never a really dirty diaper."

I was floored! In all my preparation for fatherhood and throughout my six years of being a Dad, I didn't know that such dereliction of duty was a choice. Two thoughts quickly came to mind. The first was to leverage the new knowledge to limit my involvement in the whole diaper thing. The second was to leverage this knowledge to build up IOU's to successfully negotiate a nice fishing trip somewhere. After a few moments of scheming, and understanding what my wife's response would be to the whole proposition, I reasoned that I was okay with my current job description as a dad.

I once worked for a large company where job descriptions abounded. Every time someone stepped into a new role they were handed a multi-page document that outlined all of the things the job entailed. As I look back at those early years with each of my four children, it doesn't take long for me to realize that the only things that were excluded from my list of kid-related things to do were pregnancy, delivery, and nursing.

I'm always concerned when people pick and choose how and when they will engage in parenting duties because, in a sense, they are then choosing to become parenting "specialists." Consider yourself an entrepreneur starting a new company. In order to make a go of this new venture, you have to pitch in where help is needed. The simple answer to "What is my job description?" is "What needs to be done?"

Our last daughter is out of diapers and on to accidents, but I look back at my job description and feel good that I kept it complete—including some pretty stringent diaper changing activity. Yeah, diaper changing is sometimes dirty, sometimes smelly, and lots of times not what you want to be doing. But you do get the chance to look your baby straight in the face and make them laugh, and you get to witness one of the first times that your child begins to hear and follow directions—when you teach them to lift their legs and put their hands over their heads to keep them out of the mess.

**Remember, Dad, your job description
can be summed up
in one word: Involvement.**

Some questions to think about:

- ◆ *What parenting tasks are you not looking forward to?*

- ◆ *What do your friends tell you are their favorite and least favorite parts of parenting a newborn? (If they haven't told you, go ahead and ask!)*

your space   *notes . . . thoughts . . . musings . . .*

Committed. Focused.
The "All-In" Dad

I WAS READY FOR fatherhood. I actually trained for a marathon during our first two forays into parenthood. Yes, I got in shape to get my wife pregnant and to become a parent. When I see those words on paper they seem a little nuts. Even nuttier is the distance I felt I needed to run—not 3 miles or 5 miles, but 26.2 miles. Committed. Focused. Nuts?

Do you ever watch poker on TV? One game that I love to watch is Texas Hold'em. The probability-to-win statistics on the screen are nice and some of the players are intriguing, but the best part of the whole game is when you hear those point-of-no return words, "All In." Not "I raise you" or "I call," but *all in*. It is not even my money and my heart starts to beat a little faster. It is the commitment. The focus on winning it all or winning nothing.

We had moved to a new city a year before our son was born. Shortly after he was born we moved into our first house. So I entered fatherhood without a lot of strong friendships in my new home. I was in shape, focused, and all into fathering. I started being a dad, and stopped doing almost everything else, other than an occasional golf game or weekend away with a few of the friends from my childhood.

About three years into fatherhood, I looked around and discovered that apart from my wife, I had almost completely isolated myself. I had no one who I could call and really talk. I was frustrated, lonely, 33 years old, and complaining to my wife about not having a life. My life had changed completely.

On the other hand, one of my very close friends had a colicky new baby who screamed from six to twelve hours a day. Now, this friend had always been the type of guy who liked a lot of people around, and he invited us over more than once without checking first with his wife. Despite the obvious disruption of a screaming child, he had decided that his little one wouldn't change anything about his lifestyle and choices.

Two dads. Two extremes. Both committed, focused, and all in. So who's right? As you face the changes brought on by becoming a father, there is a price to pay for living in the extremes.

Don't give up everything you once enjoyed because you're committed to a new chapter in life, and don't blow off your parenting responsibilities because you still feel entitled to play poker with the guys on Saturday nights. The key is communication between you and your wife. Figure out your priorities and talk with her about what's important for you to keep doing. Sit down with your calendars and try to find a way to work in a few activities to give yourself a break.

And remember to do the same for her! Be supportive as she tries to maintain her friendships and do the things that make her feel like a person, not just a mom. I don't think there's any magical formula here for success except to recognize up front what your priorities are (with friendships being one of them) and figuring out a way to work them into your life.

Remember, Dad, think committed, focused . . . with balance!

Some questions to think about:

- *What are three things that you will make time for after your children are born?*

- *What are three things that you will have to give up?*

your space   *notes . . . thoughts . . . musings . . .*

Love That Pediatrician!

MY WIFE IS A nurse, and therefore a very knowledgeable and informed mom while in the doctor's office. As for me, it's all I can do to keep track of the simple terms like ibuprofen, zinc oxide, and cortisone. For that reason I rarely find myself having to go to the pediatrician. That said, there was one occasion where our infant daughter had an earache, and my wife couldn't go to the doctor's office because of another commitment.

Before the visit Jenny gave me a list of things that I needed to remember so I could be an informed parent—antibiotic history (what worked and what didn't), current symptoms, and other things we had noticed. Of course, I did not write any of this down.

When I got to the appointment our doctor came in and, after getting over the surprise of seeing Dad in her exam room, began examining our daughter. After about the third question and my third answer of "I'm not really sure about that, but if it is important I can call Jenny," I realized that maybe I should have written something down.

Well, the doctor was very patient with me, and as I watched her work, listened to her questions, and watched her examine my daughter, I learned something that day: even though a baby can't tell you what they're feeling with words, they do communicate their feelings through their actions and verbal cues (that is, they flail around, pull at their ears, rub their noses and eyes, and cry like crazy). In the ten minutes it took to diagnose the problem and prescribe a solution, our pediatrician taught me that someone who can't talk can still communicate, if you know how to listen.

Your pediatrician is a key member of the team that needs to be in place when you have your first child. Don't hesitate to ask your friends for recommendations and advice when it comes to choosing the right doctor for your kids, because chances are you'll be seeing a lot of this person. And if you want to make it a successful partnership, you'll shop carefully.

Before I had kids I thought they either got sick with a cold or the flu. I was shocked and amazed at all the bugs that I have learned about along the way: parvovirus, rotavirus, hand, foot, and mouth disease. Of all the people that are going to become part of your extended parenthood team, the pediatrician is one of the most important. Listen to him or her, and be sure to write down what they tell you so you can take your kid-care cues from them. They see more kids and know more tricks than anyone.

And Remember, Dad, write down the directions!

Some questions to think about:

- *Without looking it up, what is your family pediatrician's name?*

- *Ask five fathers you know the same question. How many can answer it?*

your space   *notes . . . thoughts . . . musings . . .*

Just What You Need—
Simon Cowell in the Grocery Store

ONE DAY I ARRIVED home from work to a blissfully quiet house. That didn't last long, however, for within a few minutes, my wife, Jenny, returned from her shopping trip with the kids.

On her first trip in the door she slammed down her purse on the counter. On her second trip into the house she handed me a screaming twelve month old. On her third trip into the house our other two children were one step ahead of their mom as she complained loudly that the bagger put the bread under the bananas.

Now, I'll admit that there are times when I can't read Jenny's mind, but this wasn't one of them! My response was to grab the kids and go out the back door!

When things settled down, Jenny shared with me the following story. Her shopping trip started well with the three kids in tow. It was quite uneventful until the family reached the checkout. As they approached the line and faced the fifteen-minute checkout wait, Jenny started to field questions about that dastardly candy display. A few gentle "No, we don't need that" from Mom, and then the meltdown began.

By this point, Jenny was an expert at tuning things out and plowing ahead—but on this day she met her "Simon" in the line. For you American Idol fans, you will know Simon Cowell as the judge who gives the direct, unfiltered, and sometimes shocking feedback to the contestants. Well, on this day an elderly woman was walking past Jenny as she stood in line and, at the height of the screaming, she looked at our youngest and loudest child and said, "Would you just shut up!" Needless to say, Jenny's jaw dropped. She shot a look at this woman's husband, who quickly dropped his head and kept walking. Not wanting to make a bigger scene, Jenny decided to let it go. That was the end of the exchange.

Now if we're honest, we'll all admit to having a few "Simon" moments before our kids came along. We might not have said anything as blatant and rude as that woman, but the nonverbal signals we send are heard loud and clear (trust me on this one). You see, with kids, one thing you have to do eventually is take them out in public. And when you do, at some point in time they will not follow your directions and will act out. Sometimes you'll see looks of sympathy from other people who have been there before. Sometimes you'll catch a fleeting look of disgust. And sometimes, as my patient wife did, you'll get some verbal feedback.

My advice in this situation is to focus on the looks of sympathy or the slight smiles that indicate your troubles are triggering "I remember when" thoughts. Take comfort in the fact that you're not alone.

**Dad, remember the time
when you were Simon,
and roll with it
when you are on the other side.**

Some questions to think about:

◆ *Have you ever been irritated by someone else's children in a public place (on a plane, in a store or restaurant, etc.)? How did you react?*

◆ *Have you ever started a sentence with, "When I am a parent I'll never . . ." (now finish it)?*

your space   *notes . . . thoughts . . . musings . . .*

Don't Take It Personally, That One Year Old Doesn't Hate You

WHEN MY NIECE WAS a year old we went for a visit. I was really looking forward to holding her and playing with her. I thought she would love playing with me. After all, I was a nice "daddy type." I had four kids of my own, I smiled a lot, and I was all about getting down into their world. As soon as I saw her I was ready to dole out a big dose of uncle lovin'. But she took one look at me, started crying, and ran to her mom. I had started out too aggressively trying to interact with her, and that colored her perception of me the whole week. Other than her grabbing my leg by accident thinking it was her father's, I never was able to get her to warm up to me. Truth be told, I was hurt.

Have you ever scared a child? Did it feel like they hated you?

Dad, let me prepare you for something that I was reminded of by my little niece. Sometimes you aren't always going to be a child's first choice. Even your own kids may not prefer to be with you. Understand that sometimes the only person your child will want to be with is mom or grandma or the daycare provider. No matter what you do or how fun you are, face it, at some point you're going to be the low man on the totem pole.

Let's keep this in perspective. This is not a neighbor who has decided not to talk to you, or a coworker that you offended at the company picnic, this is an *infant*. They love to be comforted, held, fed, waited on—and sometimes they just get in their little heads that it is not going to be anyone outside a certain circle. And sometimes dad is not in that circle.

When it happens, remember two things: 1) infants don't have the capacity to hate anyone; 2) dads, uncles, and grandfathers—don't give up! Every child goes through this phase. Sometimes more than once! That's not to say it is easy—watching that look on Grandpa's face is tough, because sometimes it does hurt. When my kids were younger they would shun me every once in a while, but they came around eventually. Now my little niece is past three and warming up to me. My next strategy is bringing some candy as bait—we'll see how that works!

Remember, Dad, they don't hate you, you're just a little bit scary sometimes!

Some questions to think about:

- ◆ *What is the best greeting you have ever received from a child? How did it make you feel?*

- ◆ *Have you ever had a child shun you like I described? How did you react?*

your space   *notes . . . thoughts . . . musings . . .*

ON BEING
A BETTER SPOUSE

Rock, Paper, Scissors

ONE MEMORIAL DAY WEEKEND we were at a party where there were twenty-two kids and fourteen adults. Every child was under nine years old, and over a two-hour period there was not a single moment when at least one child wasn't crying, when there wasn't some unpleasant odor coming out of the mass of bodies, or someone wasn't being told, "Take that out of your mouth." *Relaxing* was probably not the right word for this event, even though the intent of this party was to allow for the adults to spend some "quality time" together.

In the midst of the chaos, our friend's son appeared out of the melee to present an unpleasant smelling gift to his parents. Both my friend and his wife looked at each other and said, "Your turn," almost in unison. My friend is a playful guy, so he offered one round of Rock, Paper, Scissors to determine who changed the diaper. He lost and, with a laugh, picked up his son while his wife wandered back to the party.

The point is, you'll learn a lot by watching other parents. What I witnessed in that brief moment was a great way to diffuse a potentially contentious situation by applying a simple game that most of us grew up playing. I still marvel at how fun and matter-of-fact the whole discussion was. There was no arguing about who'd done it last, or who'd done it more, or who was having the most important conversation at the moment. It was just a mutual understanding that someone had to take care of the problem; it was not convenient for either person, so they made a game out of it.

**Remember, Dad, these playful moments
are set up by first sharing the responsibilities—
then taking your chances
with Rock, Paper, Scissors!**

Some questions to think about:

- *What parenting duty would you gladly give up?*

- *What memories do you have of your parents/other parents being "playful" with each other?*

your space   *notes . . . thoughts . . . musings . . .*

The Changing
Definition of "Sexy"

THE OTHER DAY I caught myself arguing with my wife about how old I was. The pants were feeling tighter, I had been noticing some extra wrinkles and gray hair appearing, and with all of that as proof I made the comment to her that "I'm certainly not the young man that you married." When she responded that she thought I still looked "sexy," I dismissed her comment with, "Sorry, Honey, but the mirror doesn't lie. This is not sexy!"

One of my favorite books is Mitch Albom's book *The Five People You Meet in Heaven*. There is a part in the story where the main character meets his wife who had died of cancer years before. She at first appears to him in her beautiful, young form, and eventually he asks her why she looks like that. She said that she had a choice, and she thought he would like to see her young and beautiful again, not the diminished person she was after fighting cancer for several years. His response was, "Can you change it . . . to the end?" In his eyes, she carried her beauty right to the end.

Since I read that story I have been doing my own experiment—I just watch my wife. Walking, talking, cleaning, laughing, sleeping, sitting—I just watch. I look back at our wedding pictures, our honeymoon pictures, and many other albums, and just watch. You know what I have discovered? Even though it has been almost two decades since we first met, she is as beautiful today as she was the day we met. I don't see the difference.

Mitch was right. Given a choice, I want today's Jenny—not the Jenny from 1989—because as far as I'm concerned, it's the same Jenny.

So, where's all this going? Somewhere between six weeks after the baby is born and her second birthday, you're going to tell your wife how beautiful and sexy she is. When you do, there's a good chance she is going to look at you, roll her eyes, and maybe give you several examples of how her body is not what it once was. Just as I made the mirror the expert and not Jenny, your wife is going to put you in the same position. The problem: mirrors only provide a reflection of the physical person, not the whole person. The solution: describe to your wife what makes her sexy today. Let her know how you feel about her today. Tell her what you see and feel as she sits next to you today.

> **Remember, Dad, when the definition
> of sexy changes, make sure
> you update what it is
> so she understands that, too!**

Some questions to think about:

- *Do you know any older couples that surprise you with their open affection and playfulness?*

- *Have you ever heard your wife or someone else give the response I mention in this chapter? What is a good way to respond to someone who brushes off a compliment?*

your space   *notes . . . thoughts . . . musings . . .*

Wife Left You with the Baby? Okay, But That Doesn't Mean He Needs to Go to Bed at 5:30

ALL OF THE STORIES and thoughts in this book are mine . . . except this one. I asked several moms what they thought should be shared, and this is the only story that came back to me. So, here it goes—from the lips of a mom . . . .

"A few months after our first child was born, I finally settled into a routine where I could slip out to do some errands between feedings. It was a great plan, except for one problem . . . Dad. As soon as he was put in charge and the sound of the car could be heard driving away from the house, he would simply lay the baby down to go to sleep, no matter what time of day it was. When I returned, my husband would say things like, "No problem, Honey. It was easy. Piece of cake." Big win for him, big loss for me because bedtime then became 1:00 a.m.!"

Parenting is a lot like a tug-of-war or moving a heavy object; if everyone is not working in the same direction, no progress is made. I laugh at this story because in looking back, there were many times that I found myself in situations where I worked for a win for myself, but set Jenny up for a loss. I can remember watching a football game when our son was a few months old. To keep him from moving around the room, I'd lay down on the floor with him, put a pacifier in his mouth, and let him tug at my hand to keep him occupied while I watched TV. When his eyes closed it always seemed like a victory. But more often than not, it turned into trouble later.

Need some ideas to keep the game on while you're watching your child?

- ◆ How about putting your back against the couch, knees up, and cradle baby up against your legs. That way baby's looking at you and can play, but you can still keep track of the game.

- ◆ If the baby's older, slide him or her under a toy with hanging rattles or rings and watch them squeal and reach.

- ◆ See the "Get Little" chapter.

There is no greater team activity than parenting. Here is where I offer a reality check, because some of you are single fathers and don't have help. Just remember, making a child sleep now means less sleep later when you might really want or need it. For those of you who have a wife at your side, it means working together and not just making decisions that will benefit you.

Remember, Dad,
pull in the same direction as Mom!

Some questions to think about:

- *Have you ever seen this chapter acted out by another couple?*

- *How many times have you been solo with your baby in the first six months?*

- *Ask three friends who are fathers what some good activities are for keeping your baby busy and awake.*

your space   *notes . . . thoughts . . . musings . . .*

_____

_____

_____

_____

_____

_____

_____

_____

_____

_____

_____

_____

_____

_____

_____

_____

_____

_____

_____

_____

_____

_____

_____

_____

_____

_____

Your *What* Got Bigger?

AFTER CELEBRATING THE BIRTH of our second child my wife knocked me off my chair with a comment that I will never forget. She said, "Since I've started having children, my feet have gotten bigger." I had heard and experienced the "less" part of parenting—less hair, less money, less sleep, less time, less space, and did I already say less money? Certainly there are some obvious "more" things about having a baby—and if your wife asks you which ones you're referring to, just answer, "Love, toys, and love." But bigger feet? I was amused and confused at the same time over this revelation.

Many a father has said to me, "Having a child has absolutely changed my life!" When you ask for specifics, you get a variety of answers like "I want to be at home all the time" or "No matter what's gone on during the day, it all melts away when they meet me at the door." Most dads will agree that parenting is definitely life changing, but after we lose our "sympathy weight" from those late-night grocery store and fast-food runs, physically we're pretty much the same after as we were before. After hearing the feet comment from my wife, I realized that there are some things she has endured that I will never understand. All I could think about was how mad I would be if suddenly my $90 running shoes didn't fit!

As I hit mid-life and look to make my exercise routine into a habit for the second half of my life, I still wonder what it would feel like to wake up one day with bigger feet? The point of all this is that I have a theory. Part of the reason why there is such a special bond between a mom and her children is that, beyond the obvious emotional ties, moms carry with them actual physical reminders of the fact that they have brought a child or children into this world. A dad may say his life has changed after having a baby, but for a mom, quite literally everything has changed.

So what do you do with this information? First, tell her not to buy too many new shoes in the last trimester (and email me to let me know how that goes over). More importantly, somewhere along the way we have to develop empathy for our wives, so that we don't dismiss their aches and pains and body changes with one of our patented tough guy comments like, "Suck it up, Honey, this never bothered you before." (Word to the wise—don't use this one!)

And remember, Dad, be sure to love those big feet!

Some questions to think about:

- ◆ *What is the biggest sacrifice you have made as a father?*

- ◆ *How can you creatively communicate to your wife the appreciation you feel for the sacrifices she has made for your kids?*

your space   *notes . . . thoughts . . . musings . . .*

ON BEING A BETTER
SON-IN-LAW

I Can't Hear You!
Blah . . . Blah . . . Blah . . .

RECENTLY I WAS TREATED to this classic scene through my car's rear view mirror. My youngest daughter was unhappy with the direction she was getting from one of her older siblings. Being trapped in a car seat, she put her fingers in her ears, announced "I can't hear you," and started saying "Blah . . . Blah . . . Blah . . ." Eventually her sibling gave up and remained quiet.

My mother-in-law came to visit us right after our first son was born. I had no idea how to hold him, change him, or burp him, but I sure wasn't going to tell her that. I had three days to prepare for her arrival, so when she and my father-in-law came to see their first grandchild, I had my game going on—I felt like a seasoned pro. Things were going well until he cried for more than three minutes straight. Then I started shaking, sweating, and getting nervous.

My mother-in-law then gently asked me, "Can I try, Scott?" So here I was, at my moment of truth. As adults, we have learned that the finger in the ears trick is not socially acceptable. However, we have also learned that volunteering to make a quick run to the store, retreating to the other room to watch TV, or remembering the chore you have to do in the yard for the next four hours are all more subtle ways of saying "blah . . . blah . . . blah . . ."

In marriage you inherit new relationships (in-laws, new "best friends"), and with children those same relationships become more regular because everyone wants to "see the baby." Lets talk about one—the mother-in-law. I grew up listening to mother-in-law jokes. When I hear them I still think they are funny because they remind me of certain people that I have encountered over the years who would swear that those jokes reflect the norm. I know I am not supposed to laugh, but I cannot help myself.

What is it about the mother-in-law relationship that has fed material to the comedians for years? I recently read a book called *Speed of Trust* by Stephen Covey and in it he makes the point that we tend to judge ourselves by our intent, but we judge others based on their behavior. Apply this to your mother-in-law. If you ask her what her intent is, you will most likely hear, "I am just trying to help, because they need my help." If you judge them based on their behavior, it might be pretty easy to describe them as meddling, overbearing, belittling, or simply paybacks for not restraining college friends at your wedding.

So who is right? Can we agree on one point—the relationship with your mother-in-law is not an easy one because of the circumstances. After all, you stepped in as the most important person in their daughter's life, you keep her away from home on some holidays, and on top of that you got her pregnant (and let's not go into the details of that).

So how did my encounter end up? Like a seasoned pro (a mother of four), my mother-in-law had that screaming baby calm within a minute. It was impressive. I could have seen her behavior as a demonstration of superiority and a chance to show me up with her "help." I could have been extremely irritated, with years of comic strips and sitcoms as proof of her evil intentions. But I didn't. Instead I just sat back, watched, and continued to help where I could. Within twenty-four hours of coming through the door, my mother-in-law taught me the most valuable lesson I would learn in that first month—how to listen. I wanted words, I only got squeaks. With her help, I learned to decode the cries and other noises as diagnosable issues for which I had the cure. She knew what she was doing.

Let me say that I love my mother-in-law and I was fortunate to have five years to get to know her before that moment. This incident humbled me a bit and I could have been irritated, but by trusting her intent I put myself in a position to observe and learn. Some friends or family members are going to drive you nuts—but if you can get by the irritation and frustration, there are always some things to be learned.

Remember, Dad, take a deep breath, realize you might not know much, and don't run for the garage every time the going gets rough—there might be some good learning going on.

Some questions to think about:

- ◆ *Who would you have a hard time learning from?*

- ◆ *What inherited relationship do you enjoy the most? Which one is the toughest for you to deal with?*

- ◆ *Ask two other dads the questions above listen to how they deal with it?*

your space *notes . . . thoughts . . . musings . . .*

ON SURVIVING

Beware of the "Shut Up Song"

IT WAS LATE ONE night and we were in the middle of one of those no-sleep marathons. On top of that, this particular night I had stayed up a little later than normal watching a movie with the understanding that this night was going to be different than the previous thirty. Anyway, our son wasn't about to cooperate, and began screaming right on schedule—around 1:30 am. I got up with him and tried every trick I knew to get him to settle down and go back to sleep. I stood, sat, rocked, sang, walked. I held him over my shoulder, cradled him in my arms, and held him in the panther position—face down straddling one arm. I even tuned in to an Elvis movie marathon hoping that the King could work some magic. Nothing worked!

Finally, exasperated and demoralized I settled into the rocking chair and began singing what I now refer to as the "Shut Up Song." Using the "Rock-a-Bye Baby" tune I simply began singing, "Shut up, please shut up, shut up, please shut up . . . ." It was at precisely that moment that my wife Jenny walked by the door to the nursery and decided I needed a break. Her timing was perfect—it stopped me from creating new words for the next verse. I was thankful.

That was the one and only time I ever made it to the "Shut Up Song." I am not sure what your "Shut Up Song" will be, but remember that everyone has a breaking point. It's the point when you've had enough and you need to walk away for a little while. It took four children for me to figure out the one trick that works. I put the baby safely on a baby blanket on the floor for a little independent crying time while I flip on the TV to an old western that I've seen a thousand times. I pick her back up after a few minutes when we were both ready for more contact.

Remember, Dad, nobody likes to listen to or sing the "Shut Up Song."

Some questions to think about:

- ◆ *Ask two parents you know when they know they are at their breaking point.*

- ◆ *What do they do to step back from that point and reset themselves?*

your space   *notes . . . thoughts . . . musings . . .*

What's Going
to Be Your Rock?

THIS IS A STORY about late nights and early mornings—
and no, I'm not talking about those first few years after
turning twenty-one! This is called parenthood, and the
main difference here is that you have no stories to tell or
gaps to fill in the next morning.

Sixteen months into being a father, as we were pre-
paring for our second child to be born, I realized that I was
extremely dependent on a particular substance to keep me
going: caffeine. We were finishing up a tough month of
earaches, coughing, schedule interruption, and vacation.
When I took a few moments to add up my daily consump-
tion of coffee, I was staggered by the numbers. I also began
to notice that by 11:00 a.m. I was flying, by 1:30 p.m. I felt
like I had run smack into a wall. Realizing I was turning
into an addict, I stopped cold. I still remember those split-
ting headaches as I withdrew from caffeine.

I have since been through several rounds of the caf-
feine/no caffeine cycle. I have also used a regular exercise
routine, diet, and even a loud scream every now and then to
help handle the pressures that go with parenting. (Word to

the wise—do not do the scream thing in crowded elevators or grocery stores.) My perspective has changed over the years because I have regularly asked myself what is the fundamental thing in my life that will help me make it through the sleepless nights, long days, or constant interruptions to my schedule?

In other words, "What is my Rock?" That question has helped me to focus on what I regularly turn to get myself through the tough parts of being a parent. For me, I'm proud to say I've moved away from dependence on caffeine, and more toward an examination of my faith. This isn't to say that I've stopped drinking coffee, exercising, or screaming, but the thing that I rely upon for daily rejuvenation and strength is my faith. This is the Rock upon which I have built my life and the endurance and perspective that it brings me are critical for me to be a parent.

At some point in time you have to find your Rock. The questions to ask yourself when you think you have it are, "Have I come to rely on some crutch to get me through tough days and nights? Can I identify something that I can turn to at any moment and it will lift me up and allow me to persevere?" Although the answer is important, the simple habit of routinely asking yourself the question is more important. It takes most people a little time to answer this question for themselves, so the discipline of spending time thinking about this will eventually help you find the answer.

So, Dad, if you don't know it, you have to find your Rock!

Some things to think about:

- ◆ *What is your Rock?*
- ◆ *What were your parents' Rocks?*
- ◆ *Ask two dads you admire how they rejuvenate themselves.*

your space   *notes . . . thoughts . . . musings . . .*

Even Rambo Had to Rest

WHEN OUR FIRST CHILD was six months old I was sitting at work one day when the phone rang. It was my wife, Jenny, and from the first moment I heard her voice I could tell she was in pain. In fact, she had been out on the front porch moving a plant and had thrown her back out. She had managed to get into the house and to the phone, but she couldn't move, and she was lying there watching our little man rolling on the floor in front of her.

Of course, I quickly drove home to help. Finally, a situation in which I was being called on to do something she couldn't do. I kind of saw myself as Rambo, the guy who always faced incredible odds on the movie screen, but battled his way to victory! After a (relatively) quick trip to the emergency room and a stop by the pharmacy for some medicine, I was ready to take on baby, house, and anything else that had to be done. Like Rambo, I was going to conquer whatever the world and our baby threw at me. I steeled myself for the battle; I had been training my entire life for this moment.

The first twenty-four hours were a blur—meals, cleaning, constantly attending to baby, bringing him to

Jenny to feed . . . it seemed like one thing after another until the day was gone. After two days of me on high alert and leading the patrol, my sister-in-law came over and offered to do the laundry and some cleaning so I could rest. I respectfully declined her offer of help. After all, I had everything under control and was ready for more. John Rambo had nothing on me!

Within a few hours of her leaving I was sitting in front of my injured wife, broken down into tears, telling her that I was overwhelmed and I had nothing left. I can honestly say that after four children this was the one and only time that I had a reason to be more tired and stressed than she was!

I will never forget that moment. For 48 hours I had stared into the face of what my wife did every single day. Walking in her footsteps brought me to my knees.

There were several lessons that I learned that day, but the one I remember is the downside of being driven by pride. Pride can be a good thing, but when it comes to parenting it can lead us down a bumpy road. My pride drove me to forego an offer of help and led me to a place where total collapse was the only possible outcome. The key is to ask for help (this speaks to both dads and moms) before the request emerges weakly from the haggard form of a person in the fetal position on a couch. At that point it becomes an emergency, not a situation that can be managed.

Remember, Dad,
even Rambo had to rest!

Some questions to think about:

- ◆ *What life situation has emotionally or physically stretched you the most?*

- ◆ *How well and how often do you ask for help?*

- ◆ *How do you reenergize after a long day?*

your space   *notes . . . thoughts . . . musings . . .*

The One Thing . . . Love

REMEMBER THE BILLY CRYSTAL movie *City Slickers*? In it Billy's character is having a conversation with Jack Palance, playing a crusty old cowboy named Curly. In summary, Billy's character was trying to absorb some wisdom from this seasoned older man and asked him "Do you know what the secret to life is?" Curly's reply: "One thing. Just one thing. You stick to that and the rest don't mean s——!"

Have you ever had one of those moments where suddenly a complex topic was summarized into one statement that encapsulated the issue perfectly? This is one such example.

Early on in my fathering journey I was listening to an eight hour tape series about being a good father, husband, etc. In his final comments the author shared a story about an experiment done in a Russian orphanage in the middle part of the 20th century. A group of orphan babies were fed and changed but not held at all. Over 80% of them died. Another group that was fed the same but held and loved everyday had the opposite result—they thrived.

Now, this isn't the kind of research experiment that you want to conduct in your own home, certainly. But it points to the fact that babies thrive when they have someone to hold them, talk to them, and let them experience a warm embrace. What a strong message for us!

So how do you ensure that your child will thrive? Hopefully this book has given you some ideas. Loving the kids, loving their mother, loving the friends that you have around you . . . it all matters. If you are a father who does not live with your children, or is raising them without their mother—your love might look a little different and your "to love" list might be a little different, but your task is still the same.

Remember, Dad, it's nice to feel the love inside, but those people in your life (especially the little ones) need to *see* and *feel* the love through your actions.

Some questions to think about:

- *What is one way your father/mother showed love toward you that you want to do with your children?*

- *What is one way to show love that you never received as a child that you would like to provide your children?*

your space *notes . . . thoughts . . . musings . . .*

The End—or, maybe for you—
The Beginning

All books end somewhere. It doesn't seem right to end this book, because the topic you have chosen to read about, the role you have chosen to take on, is just beginning.

Being a father is great! It's a privilege! And it also can be a little bit overwhelming at times. That's why you should not do it alone. Having other fathers to connect with, to get some advice from, or to just unload thoughts and frustrations has been so critical for me over the past twelve years. If this book was a gift from another father, they cared enough to buy it for you, so take them up on the offer (or make the offer yourself) to spend some time talking with them. Not sure what to talk about? Start with sports, the weather, work, and then at some point use the chapters in this book to bring up your fatherhood questions.

I am also here to listen. On my Web site, www.momentsforfathers.com, I have provided a way for you to share your stories with me and have access to a blog where I will continue sharing my observations with you. As a father of four and a husband of one, I am still learning myself, and part of my reason for writing this book was to start a conversation with other dads so I could continue to grow into the role I took on over a decade ago.

Also, use the space in this book to jot down some thoughts on the chapters that hit home for you, and use the blank pages at the end of this book to record some of your favorite "aha" moments from being a dad. One thing I'm absolutely certain about being a father: the time goes by very quickly. Not long ago I had the chance to hold a newborn, and as I cradled that eight pound child I had a hard time believing that it has been over four years since I held my own baby.

**Dad, time is passing—get to it,
look for some help along the way,
and, above all, remember:
Sometimes, you just have to laugh.**

About the Author

Scott Patchin's sense of humor about life started somewhere between his first practical joke (plastic spider in the refrigerator—sorry Mom) and his third year at Michigan Tech University, where he was studying to become an engineer, of all things. His journey into teaching and helping others reach their goals began almost two decades ago as he began volunteering to lead a Junior Achievement program. Since that first moment, he has been working to make this passion a career. Through his roles as a teaching assistant, adjunct professor, corporate trainer, and career coach, Scott has touched many people with his passion for teaching and developing others.

In the middle of his journey to teaching he became a father, and it was his sense of humor and commitment to learning that carried him through those first few years of fatherhood. Helping others to gain the wisdom and perspective that a new father needs is an extension of his own personal mission, which is "to be a guide for others so they realize the excellence they were born to achieve." *So You're Gonna Be a Dad—Now What?* is his first book in a series called the Moments Series for Fathers, developed to help fathers make the most of the moments they are given, and to encourage them to create some on their own.

Scott lives with his wife, Jenny, and their four children in Michigan. When he is not being a husband, father, or friend, he is enjoying the outdoors through running, fishing, kayaking, or tending to his vegetable garden. Scott has successfully completed twelve 25K races, six marathons, and one 50K ultramarathon—but his enjoyment from running has always centered around the time spent training and talking with his running partners.

Writing Your Own Stories

Finally, I have finished writing this book, but my guess is that you have only just begun to write yours. I have added extra pages at the end for you to jot down your own stories. I encourage you to at least jot down some notes because the memories you have of being a dad are going to be so numerous that you may find you're hard-pressed to remember them all. My wish for you is that at some time, way down the road, you will be able to hand this book over to a son or son-in-law and begin to have the conversation with them that I am inviting you to have now.

my stories

my stories

my stories

my stories